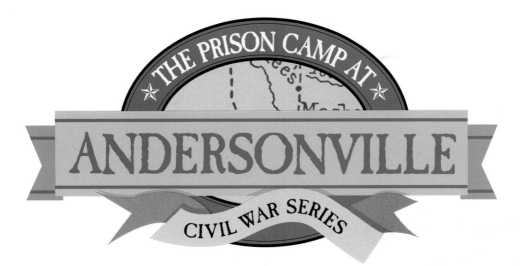

THE PRISON CAMP AT
ANDERSONVILLE
CIVIL WAR SERIES

TEXT BY WILLIAM G. BUR~

Thanks to Fred Sanchez, Joan Burnett and the interpretive staff at A~   ~istoric Site.

Published by Eastern National, copyright 1995.

Eastern National provides quality educational products and services to the visitors
to America's national parks and other public trusts.

Cover: Detail of a drawing by Thomas O'Dea, a former prisoner at Andersonville. (NPS)

Back cover: Photograph of the Providence Spring Memorial at Andersonville National Historic Site. (NPS)

To order additional titles in the Civil War Series or other national park-related items,
please call 1-800-821-2903, or visit our online store at www.eParks.com.

THE PRISON CAMP AT ANDERSONVILLE

Included in this book are short histories of the other Civil War prison camps and entries from the diaries of some of the prisoners.

*I*n the very beginning of the Civil War, prisoners of war were exchanged right on the battlefield, a private for a private, a sergeant for a sergeant and a captain for a captain. In 1862 this system broke down and caused the creation of large holding pens for prisoners in both the North and South. On July 18, 1862, Major General John A. Dix of the Union Army met with the Confederate representative, Major General Daniel H. Hill, and a cartel was drafted providing for the parole and exchange of prisoners. This draft was submitted to and approved by their superiors. Four days later, the cartel was formally signed and ratified, and became known as the Dix-Hill Cartel.

The Dix-Hill Cartel failed by mid-year, for reasons including the refusal of the Confederate Government to exchange or parole black prisoners. They threatened to treat black prisoners as slaves and to execute their white officers. There was also the problem of prisoners returning too soon to the battlefield. When Vicksburg surrendered on July 4, most of those Confederate prisoners who

were paroled were back in the trenches within weeks.

The discussions on exchange lasted until October 23, 1862, when Secretary of War Edwin M. Stanton directed that all commanders of places of confinement be notified that there would be no more exchanges. This decision would greatly affect the large numbers of prisoners in northern and southern prison camps. The so-called "holding pens" now became permanent prisons. Among the prisoner-of-war camps in the North were Camp Douglas in Chicago and Johnson's Island and Camp Chase in Ohio. In the South were Libby Prison and Belle Isle in Richmond and Camp Florence in South Carolina.

Through the latter part of 1863, the two prisons in Richmond became overcrowded. This condition plus severe food shortages made Confederate officials look for a more suitable location to build a prison. Their search took them south, far from the fighting around Richmond.

Captain W. Sidney Winder was selected to find a suitable location in Southwest Georgia. When Winder reached Milledgeville, the Georgia capital, Governor Joseph E. Brown introduced him to members of the legislature from the southwest counties of Georgia. Winder proceeded to Albany, but property owners discouraged him. He then traveled to Americus, where Uriah Harrold, a purchasing agent for the Commissary Department, informed him of Andersonville on the Southwestern

AFTER THE CARTEL OF EXCHANGE HAD BEEN AGREED UPON, AIKEN'S LANDING ON THE JAMES RIVER IN VIRGINIA WAS MADE A POINT FOR EXCHANGE IN THE EAST. COMMISSIONERS MET WITH PRISONERS BROUGHT FROM EITHER RICHMOND OR FT. MONROE, EXCHANGED ROLLS, AND WORKED THEIR EXCHANGES. THEY HAD A TABLE OF EQUIVALENTS IN WHICH THE PRIVATE WAS THE BASIC UNIT OF EXCHANGE.

(USAMHI)

Railroad. According to Winder the location had a "large supply of beautiful clear water."

In evaluating the area, Winder settled on the site in the third week of December 1863. The property was in Sumter County (now part of Macon County), five miles west of the Flint River and 1,600 feet east of the Andersonville Depot. There were approximately twenty people living in the town of Andersonville, so opposition to the prison was nil. The property owner, Benjamin B. Dykes, received $50.00 per year for the use of the land. The site was selected and named Camp Sumter for the county it was located in. Soon the prison was simply known as Andersonville.

With the site selected, the next step was to begin construction. The responsibility belonged to the Quartermaster Department. Selected for the job was Richard B. Winder of Maryland, a cousin of Captain W. Sidney Winder and a nephew of Brigadier General John H. Winder, who was provost marshal general of the Richmond area and would later oversee all

prison camps in the Confederacy east of the Mississippi.

In January 1864 the work began, with slaves digging the ditch and felling the trees for a prison that would house 10,000 prisoners. The pine trees were cut

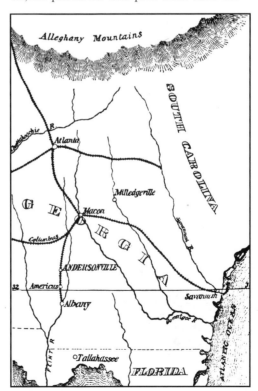

A PERIOD MAP OF THE ANDERSONVILLE REGION.

(LC)

3

LIBBY PRISON

*L*ibby Prison was located in Richmond, Virginia, in a building which was incorrectly called a tobacco warehouse. It was originally the establishment of William Libby & Son, Ship Chandlers, 20th & Cary Streets. It was a four-story building containing eight rooms. The men slept on the floor. There was a water closet on each floor that became a privy which rendered foul air and polluted the entire building. The prison was opened in April 1861 and was closed in April 1865. The total number of prisoners held during its existence was approximately 25,000. This was primarily an officers' prison.

The prisoners cooked their own rations with inadequate fuel, the rations furnished were inadequate, and there was a shortage of clothing and blankets. Rations consisted of beef, bacon, flour, beans, rice and vinegar. Of those who died at Libby, 6,276 are buried in a cemetery in Henrico County southeast of Richmond, two miles from the city and one and a half miles from the James River. There are 817 known graves and 5,459 unknown. Some of the bodies came from Belle Isle, Hollywood, Oakwood and the poorhouse cemeteries in Richmond.

(CHICAGO HISTORICAL SOCIETY)

to twenty-two feet in length with five feet set in the ground and seventeen feet standing above the ground. The slaves used broad axes to make all sides flat so that the prisoners could not see the outside of the prison. The stockade was built with two gates, the South Gate and the North Gate. By the time the stockade was completed in the third week of March, there were eighty sentry boxes at forty yard intervals. The prison interior also had a deadline which was about nineteen feet from the stockade wall. The guards had orders to shoot any prisoners who walked across the deadline.

Initially, the guards were members of the 55th Georgia, commanded by Lt. Colonel Alexander W. Persons, and the

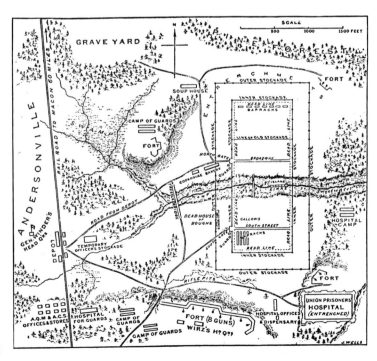

PLAN OF THE STOCKADE AND SURROUNDINGS AT ANDERSONVILLE FROM *CENTURY MAGAZINE*.

26th Alabama. Their stay at Camp Sumter was temporary. Brigadier General Howell Cobb was ordered to command the newly authorized Reserve Corps of Georgia. He established his headquarters at Macon and proceeded to enlist guards for Andersonville. In the beginning of May the first two regiments of Georgia Reserves arrived at the post, and the two veteran regiments were relieved to take part in the spring offensive of General Joseph E. Johnston's Army of Tennessee. The third regiment of Georgia Reserves reached Andersonville on May 11. Most of the new guards were old men or young boys with a smattering of veterans who had been wounded in battle.

The first batch of prisoners, 500 strong, arrived on February 25 (some accounts say prisoners arrived the 24th), and were turned into the stockade even though it stood unfinished and food and equipment were in short supply. Before authorities could get the situation in hand and get the prison into proper order, they were swamped by an unceasing influx of prisoners, some 400 arriving every day.

Food and containers to hold rations were in short supply. Prisoner Charles C. Fosdick, Co. K, 5th Iowa Infantry stated, "We were put to our wit's end to know how to receive our rations. We had no vessels except our little coffee cans, and many did not have even these. Some would draw in their hats, mixing meal, peas and beef all together; others would tear out a shirt sleeve, tie a string around one end, and draw in it, and others would draw theirs in a corner of their blouse." During the month of March the rations consisted of cornmeal, beans and an occasional ration of meat. As the prisoners kept pouring into the stockade this ration gradually diminished.

The prisoners were divided into detachments of 270 men. They were again subdivided into three companies of ninety men each with a sergeant in charge. They received their rations through their sergeant who divided them as equally as he could. By the end of

LOUISIANA ZOUAVE PRISONERS IN THE GUARD-HOUSE AT FORTRESS MONROE.

(*HARPER'S WEEKLY*)

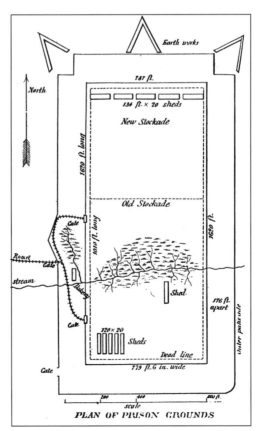

PLAN OF PRISON GROUNDS, ANDERSONVILLE, THE STOCKADE, MEASURED BY DR. HAMLIN IN THE SUMMER OF 1865.

IN 1994 TO COMMEMO-
RATE THE 130TH
ANNIVERSARY OF
ANDERSONVILLE
PRISON, THE NATIONAL
PARK SERVICE PRE-
SENTED A LIVING HISTO-
RY PROGRAM TO RECRE-
ATE LIFE AT THE
PRISON.

(NPS)

able and would be an object of pain for the rest of his life.

By April 1, the stockade designed for 10,000 men held 7,160 prisoners. Between that date and the 8th of May, 5,787 men arrived from various places; 728 died, 13 escaped and 7 were recaptured, making a total of 12,213 inmates. As Richard Winder was to admit later, he had made a grievous error in placing the bakery and cookhouse upstream from the prison. They polluted the stream that the prisoners used for drinking and bathing.

Death came from the introduction of contagious diseases into the camp, pollution of the prisoners' drinking water within the stockade, inadequate hospital accommodations, the lack of prisoner quarters, exposure to the elements, bad sanitary practices, short and defective rations and overcrowding. Upon their arrival the first prisoners saw that there was no shelter from the elements, so

March, there was "nothing but corn meal and a little salt."

It was on March 27 that Captain Henry Wirz was ordered to Andersonville to take charge of the inside of the prison and all of the prisoners. Heinrich Hartmann Wirz was born November 25, 1823, in Zurich, Switzerland. His interests lay in the medical field, and he did have some medical training, but his father objected and insisted that he enter the mercantile field. He sailed to America in 1849. When the Civil War began he joined the 4th Louisiana Infantry and was wounded during the battle of Seven Pines. The wound was incur-

A SKETCH OF
PRISONERS RECEIVING
RATIONS, FROM *LIFE
AND DEATH IN REBEL
PRISONS*, BY ROBERT H.
KELLOGG, 1866.

CAPTAIN HENRY WIRZ

Henry Wirz was born on November 25, 1823, in Zurich, Switzerland and was educated in Italy and Zurich. He emigrated to the United States in 1849 and in 1854 was married in Kentucky to a widow with two children. They had one child from their union. The family moved to Louisiana, and when the Civil War broke out he joined Company A, 4th Battalion, Louisiana Volunteers. He was given a battlefield commission in the battle of Seven Pines where his right arm was shattered and

was not to completely heal for the rest of his life. After his exploits at Seven Pines he was made a captain and was

assigned to work for General Winder, superintendent of military prisons. He first worked at Libby Prison in Richmond and then, in July 1862, he was sent to command the Confederate Prison at Tuscaloosa, Alabama. Because of Wirz' nationality and education, President Davis made him a special minister and sent him to Europe to carry secret dispatches to the Confederate Commissioners. He returned from Europe in January of 1864 and on April 12, 1864, he arrived at Andersonville, Georgia, to command the military prison there.

they constructed what they called "she-bangs." The prisoners constructed huts and lean-tos from logs, limbs, shrubs and brush left within the prison.

They also used blankets, tent flies, overcoats and clothing from the dead. Some prisoners used the prison yard to make bricks which when placed one upon the other became their shebangs. There was no effort in the beginning by the Confederate administration or the prisoners themselves to properly design or lay out streets, so the shebangs went in all directions. This disorganization and lack of proper camp administration probably led to a higher mortality rate.

Many of the letters, manuscripts and diaries written during and after this prison experience spoke of the same things: the loneliness, dejection and the complete gloom of despairing individuals. G.E. Reynolds, Co. F, 86th Ohio Infantry, recalled his arrival at Andersonville by writing, "As the heavy wooden door closed behind us my heart sank within me, and hope which till that time had

buoyed me up, fled. And such a sense of utter and hopeless desolation crept over me as I hope never to feel again." Asa Isham, Co. F, Michigan Cavalry, wrote, "Until now, we have not believed that the government we had voluntarily

AN ILLUSTRATION OF CITIZENS VIEWING THE CAMP.

(NPS)

March 27, 1864

Sometimes we have visitors of citizens and women who come to look at us. There is sympathy in some of their faces and in some a lack of it.

John L. Ransom Sergeant, Co. A, 9th Michigan Cavalry

SERGEANT JOHN L. RANSOM WAS ONE OF MANY PRISONERS WHO KEPT DIARIES.

joined in protecting could abandon us, after faithful service, to the tender mercies of our enraged and barbarous enemies."

The officials at the prison had a great need for lumber and tools so that they could erect some type of barracks and other facilities for the prisoners. But most of the lumber that arrived was used for building outside of the prison.

The following letter was written by R.B. Winder, captain and assistant quartermaster at Andersonville, to Major J.G. Michaeloffsky, quartermaster at Macon, Georgia on April 11, 1864:

SIR: Captain Armstrong brings me the information that a train load of lumber has been waiting transportation at Gordon for the last twelve days. The great want and emergency for this lumber at this post requires it of me to ask you to exercise your official authority in placing it here at the earliest possible moment. The instructions forwarded to post quartermasters in relation to Government transportation fully warrant your taking the most decided and prompt action in this case. The very great emergency, as far as the need of it here requires, safely excuses me in requiring you to act in this matter. I am burying the dead without coffins. I shall rely entirely upon you. If it is not here in a reasonable period I shall be compelled to report the matter to the authorities at Richmond.

The problems with obtaining lumber even affected sanitation at the prison camp. Captain Wirz came up with a very good idea for the problem of the sewage and the "sinks," toilets in modern terms. He planned to build two dams across the stream running through the stockade and open those dams and flush out the bottom end of the stream daily. It could have worked, but both lumber and tools were hard to acquire and other projects vied for attention.

In May, 708 prisoners died. According to the Confederate adjutant general there were 12,000 prisoners on the 16 1\2 acres, with at least 500 arriving each day. The stream, "Stockade Branch," was fast becoming a quagmire. Prisoner

A PHOTO OF THE "PRISONERS" FROM THE NPS LIVING HISTORY PROGRAM.

(NPS)

Charles Chesterman, Co. A, 13th US Infantry, was to write, "All of the filth from the prison ran into the creek and we had to strain the water through our teeth to keep the maggots out."

There were 1,200 guards, four pieces of artillery and a cavalry company, so the chance of escape was extremely small. Even the guards spoke about the excessive heat for May. In this heat the prisoners suffered from many types of diseases. Dr. Josiah H. White did everything in his power to alleviate the condition of the suffering patients.

It was in the beginning of May that Dr. R.R. Stevenson superseded Dr. White as medical director. In a letter to Major Thomas P. Turner in Richmond he said, "I wish to add a word in relation to the officer commanding the interior of the prison, Captain Wirz, who, in my opinion, deserves great credit for the good sense and energy he has displayed in the man-agement of the prison at Andersonville. He is the only man who seems to fully comprehend his important duties." He went on to say that two commissioned officers should be assigned to assist him.

Captain Wirz reported on May 8 that he had received axes and spades from Columbus, Georgia, and would have everything in the interior of the prison completed in two weeks. In the same letter he said, "I am here in a very unpleasant position growing out of the rank that I now hold and suggest the propriety of being promoted. Having full control of the prison consequently of the daily prison guard, the orders which I have to give are very often not obeyed with the promptness the occasion requires, and I am of opinion that it emanates from the reluctance of obeying an officer who holds the same rank as they do."

Now authorities were advised to

NOTHING COULD MATCH IN NOTORIETY THIS PLACE IN SOUTHWEST GEORGIA OFFICIALLY KNOWN AS CAMP SUMTER. IN AUGUST 1864 SOUTHERN PHOTOGRAPHER A.J. RIDDLE TOOK THE ONLY KNOWN PHOTOGRAPHS OF ANDERSONVILLE PRISON. THIS PHOTOGRAPH SHOWS THE NORTHWEST VIEW OF THE STOCKADE. THE DEATH RATE THAT SUMMER WAS WELL OVER 100 PER DAY.

(LC)

April 25, 1864

On the 21st the tunnel was opened and two fellows escaped to the outside. Myself next went out— jumped up and ran for dear life. In an hour we had traveled perhaps three miles. We heard dogs after us. Capt. Wirz interviewed us. We were put in the chain gang—not so bad at all. We had more to eat than when inside. Am not permenently hurt any.

John L. Ransom

with Andersonville than any place they have been since they were captured. They are now living bountiful on the very best that Southwestern Georgia can afford. Their daily ration consist of 1/3 of a pound of good ham or bacon and 1 1/2 pounds of meal. They also get peas and sometimes fresh and pickled beef. The patients in the hospital, in addition to ham and meal, get rice flour, potatoes, chickens and eggs."

On May 8 John Ransom wrote in his diary, "We get a quarter of a loaf of bread, weighing about six ounces, and four or five ounces of pork." After rations were issued each day, there would be a general meeting of densely packed prisoners, all trying to trade for something more palatable, or for that which they had not gotten. Some would cry out, "Who will trade salt for wood? Who will trade wood for beans?" At this time Howell Cobb reported, "The duties of the inside command are admirably performed by Captain Wirz, whose place it would be difficult to fill. I

move the hospital from the inside of the prison to the outside and furnish enough tents for 1,000 patients. There was insufficient room for the prisoners, much less for the hospital patients. Also, plans were being made to enlarge the stockade in the very near future.

On May 7 the *Macon Telegraph* newspaper reported, "Mr. Fidderman informed me that the prisoners unanimously express themselves much better pleased

CAMP CHASE

Camp Chase, located in Columbus, Ohio, was a training camp for newly inducted recruits, but it also became a prison camp for Confederate prisoners. The first prisoners arrived in July 1861 and the camp closed after the war. During its existence it held 9,416 prisoners and had 650 guards. Water was obained from wells 15-20 feet deep. The sinks consisted of a ditch which ran across the prison. Wood for cooking was delivered within the camp at three sticks per man per day. Rations consisted of bacon, beef, coffee, sugar and one loaf of bread each per day.

The wooden stockade—700 feet long and 300 feet wide—was smaller than the one at Andersonville. The prisoners were housed in barracks. During the time the prison was open 2,200 men died. They were buried in the prison cemetery which today is cared for by the United Daughters of the Confederacy.

(NA)

(OHIO HISTORICAL SOCIETY)

May 15, 1864

Sunday comes again. But, oh what a place to spend the Sabbath. No chiming bells. Nothing to put us in the mind of this being the Lords day, OH! How I long to be at home once more (and) go to church every Sunday.

Leander W. Kennedy, Co. I, 5th Michigan Infantry

still think the rank of the commanding officer of the post should be a Brigadier-General."

Many occupations were taken up by the prisoners, not only to kill time but to make money for their needs. There were bakers, bucketmakers and kettlemakers. Most of the raw materials were smuggled in since the guards had a fondness for Yankee greenbacks. John Ransom's diary entry on May 22 reveals that he had taken up laundering with a Minnesota Indian named Batiste.

According to a report dated May 10 from the adjutant general's office, Captain Wirz was trying to implement his idea of draining the swamp area to make it more habitable for the prisoners. There would be an upper dam for drinking and a lower one for bathing. One million feet of lumber had been ordered; but there was no way to transport the lumber to the prison. Two squads of prisoners of twenty-five each were detailed every day, supplied with shovels and charged with the duty of removing from the encampment all offal, the combustible part of which was burned and the rest thrown into the stream.

Prisoners had been allowed outside

CAMP DOUGLAS

Camp Douglas, located in Chicago, Illinois, became a prisoner-of-war camp in February 1862 when General U.S. Grant captured Fort Donelson and sent between 8,000 and 9,000 captured Confederates to the prison. Over the course of its existence the prison housed upwards of 30,000.

The prisoners stayed in barracks. The prison had an inadequate sanitary system, sometimes poor food, not enough clothing or blankets, inept and inaccurate record keeping, confused leadership and oftentimes cruel discipline. Death came from diseases such as typhus, dysentery and small-

pox, but mostly from the cold. A total of 3,759 prisoners died at Camp Douglas. They were buried at Oak Woods Cemetery. Located within the cemetery is the Confederate

Mound Monument, which notes that this is the largest burial site for Southern soldiers in the North.

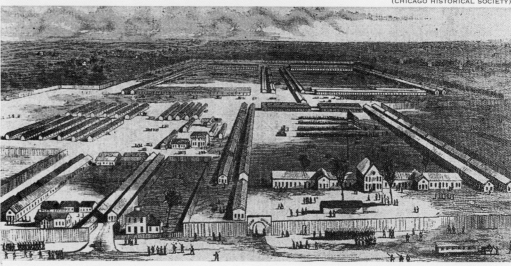

May 25, 1864

In the early summer, Captain Wirz issued to the prisoners picks and shovels, with which to dig wells for increased water supply. From some of these wells the men started tunnels through which to escape. Discovering this, the commander withdrew the tools, and ordered the wells to be filled up.

John L. Maile
Co. F, 8th
Michigan Infantry

of the prison to collect wood and pine boughs for their shebangs, but the intimacy between the guards and prisoners became so great, the practice had to be discontinued. The prisoners were allowed to receive boxes of food from outside after a careful inspection of the contents. They also were allowed to receive and send mail subject to the post commander's approval. A letter box was installed inside the stockade. If a box was received for a prisoner who had died, the box was given to hospital authorities for distribution.

By mid-May the guards numbered 1,193. Artillery consisted of four guns: two 10-pounders, rifled, and two Napoleons. Both sets of guns were on hills commanding the two prison gates and the interior of the prison. The number of men detailed for guard duty each day was: commissioned officers, 7; noncommissioned officers, 16; privates, 280; total 303, exclusive of artillery. The guard was posted as follows: one man in each sentry box on the top of the stockade, forty men at each gate in the day and eighty at night. The remainder were posted around the stockade, fifty yards from the wall.

The hospital was divided into two

divisions, with a full surgeon in charge of each. One of these divisions was subdivided into three wards and the other into two. Each ward was under the care of an assistant surgeon. Numerous prisoners were detailed as nurses and hospital stewards for all purposes. A surgeon was appointed each day as professional officer of the day whose duty it was to see that the hospital was well policed and that the nurses and stewards discharged their duties promptly and efficiently. This officer was required to make a daily morning report.

The diseases most prevalent among the prisoners were dysentery and diarrhea. About one mile from the prison was the smallpox hospital. On the 20th of May, the hospital was moved from inside the prison to outside the stockade. It was located in a stand of timber on two acres of land to the southeast of the main enclosure. It was enclosed by a board fence about six feet in height and was laid out in regular streets, or wards. The hospital was supplied with water from a creek that ran through the southwest corner and was unadulterated with the filth and garbage of either the rebel camps or the prison pen.

Escape was a constant topic of conversation among the prisoners and many attempts were made. Some prisoners attempted to tunnel out while others would run away when outside the stockade on detail. One ingenious prisoner pretended to be dead, had two friends carry him out to the dead house and after dark just got up and ran

away. Afterwards, Wirz, suspecting the trick, had a surgeon inspect the bodies before permitting them out for burial.

Life within the enclosure became a routine, except for tricks that were played on the guards. When a prisoner died, the rest of the men in the detachment would hide the fact from the guards as long as possible so that they could get the dead man's ration. Many prisoners would be counted two or three times by the sergeant to hide the deaths. Also, when a prisoner died his friend would tie a strong piece of cord to the dead man with the other end tied to himself so that no one would steal the corpse during the night. Carrying his

PRISONERS BEING ISSUED RATIONS AND TRADING FOR SOMETHING MORE PALATABLE.

(NPS)

13

RUNNING PARALLEL AND NEXT TO THE STREAM THAT PROVIDED DRINKING WATER WERE THE LONG SINKS OR LATRINES, AS SHOWN IN THIS 1864 PHOTOGRAPH BY A.J. RIDDLE.

(NA)

friend to the dead house would enable him to pick up a piece of wood the next day for cooking his food.

On May 21 the *Sumter Republican* reported, "The Andersonville prisoners nearly escaped. The commander discovered the plans. At this time there are 17,000 prisoners there and 500 are being added every day. They cannot be turned loose upon the people. 3,000 to 5,000 men are needed to keep them but there are only 500 men there. Col. Persons is aware of the problem. West Georgia is the Egypt of the Confederacy and the crops must not be destroyed." Also, the *Macon Telegraph* reported, "It will be too late to cry 'Wolf' when they have made their escape, and

are sacking every smoke house in the country, cutting telegraph wire, burning government stores, destroying railroad bridges, killing stocks, etc."

Many of the Andersonville prisoners who arrived in the stockade in April and May were well supplied with money. The Federal armies were reclothed and paid off in the spring of 1864 for the spring campaigns. Many of the new recruits and reenlisted veterans had bounty money with them when captured. Greenbacks could be pressed into the sole of a shoe, or placed inside a brass button. Money was concealed about the person in various ways. Some swallowed their rings and others put their money into bowls of large Dutch pipes with a little tobacco sprinkled on top. When searched, they would pretend to be busy lighting their pipes and thus escape suspicion. Gambling was carried on quite extensively; faro, dice, and $10.00 stakes were commonly played for. Trade was carried on with the guards on the outside of the wall by talking through the cracks and throwing articles over the fence. Another trade was carried on as well, as noted by prisoner John

MOST OF THE GUARDS AFTER EARLY MAY WERE MEMBERS OF THE GEORGIA RESERVES. THESE WERE MOSTLY OLD MEN OR YOUNG BOYS.

(NPS LIVING HISTORY PROGRAM)

JOHN H. WINDER

*J*ohn H. Winder was born February 21, 1800, in Somerset County, Maryland. He graduated from West Point in 1820 and taught artillery tactics there until 1823 when he resigned. He reentered the service in 1827 and fought with distinction in the Seminole War. He was brevetted major for gallantry at Contreras and Churubusco, and lieutenant-colonel for gallantry in the attack upon Mexico during the Mexican-American War. Winder resigned his Federal commission in April 1861, when the Civil War began, and the following June was commissioned a brigadier general in the

Confederate army, with the appointment to provost marshal and commander of prisons in Richmond. Later he was given command of the Department of Henrico. In 1864, after the largest number of enlisted men had been transferred to Andersonville and many of the officers to Macon, he was placed in charge of all the prisons in Alabama and Georgia. He made his headquarters at Andersonville and arrived in June 1864. The following September he transferred his base to Camp Lawton at Millen, Georgia, and on November 21 was made commander of all Confederate prisons east of the Mississippi. He did not survive the war and died February 6, 1865, probably of a heart attack.

Northrup, Co. D, 7th Connecticut Infantry: "There is one commodity never had in any market. It is ahead of any Dutch brewery extract; it is meal beer made by letting corn meal sour in water. The vendor cries, 'here is your nice meal beer, right sour, well seasoned with sassafras.'"

R. B. Winder, in his report to General

THE SOUTH GATE HAD A GUARD HOUSE AND SENTRY TOWERS ON EACH SIDE AND SERVED AS THE SICK CALL AREA WHERE MEDICAL OFFICERS WERE POSTED.

(LC)

Winder on May 25 stated, "And if the number of prisoners is very much increased and this camp made, as I suppose it will be, the grand receptacle for prisoners captured throughout the Confederacy, then I would by all means recommend that another area be enclosed with a stockade similar to the present one and that the grounds selected be on a stream about one-quarter of a mile south of the present camp." He went on to write, "Immediate arrangements should be made in which the prisoners may be sheltered from the rains and protected from the heat of the sun. Buildings should be commenced as soon as practicable for the winter, and in the meantime tents should be furnished for their use during the summer. Without this they will die off by hundreds, and will be a dead loss to us in the way of exchange."

Although it never bore fruition, Captain Winder planned to install a shoe factory at the prison. He had trouble find-

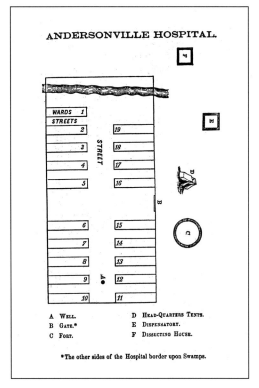

ANDERSONVILLE HOSPITAL.

WARDS 1
STREETS 2
3
4
5

STREET

6
7
8
9
10

19
18
17
16

15
14
13
12
11

A   WELL.   D   HEAD-QUARTERS TENTS.
B   GATE.*   E   DISPENSATORY.
C   FORT.   F   DISSECTING HOUSE.

*The other sides of the Hospital border upon Swamps.

May 27, 1864

We twist up pieces of tin, stovepipe, etc. for dishes, A favorite and common dish is half of a canteen. Our spoons are made of wood. Hardly one man in ten has a dish of any kind to put his rations of soup or molasses in, and often old shoes, dirty caps are brought into requisition.

John L. Ransom

ing tools and leather for this endeavor. In his report he wrote, "It will not answer to commence operations until every branch of the department was properly furnished both with tools and stock, a sufficient quantity of the latter being particularly required; without, the workmen would be idle in a very few days."

Food was always paramount in the prisoners' minds. Every day they thought about food and at night they dreamt about food. In his diary W.F. Lyon, Co. C, 9th Minnesota Infantry wrote, "It was Sunday; we were seated at the table; my brother sat opposite me, and my father opposite my mother. In the middle of the table, which was covered with a clean, white cloth, sat a plate of mother's biscuits. I couldn't wait for the blessing, but reached over and took one from the plate. Holding it up, I said, 'In Andersonville, three biscuits like this would have been worth a dollar.' Just as I was about to put it to my mouth I awoke. Imagine my disappointment."

On June 3 one of the prisoners wrote, "A number of the 54th Massachusetts regiment, and some others, were already of our number, and they were universally treated better than we white soldiers. They were taken outside every day to perform some labor, and allowed double rations, and also the privilege of buying things outside and bringing them into the prison at evening, and selling them to such as had any money, for a good round price in greenbacks."

There were also many cases of insane, helpless and entirely naked men inside the prison. Often, when a prisoner became helpless, gang members known as the "Raiders" would rob him. The boldness of the Raiders grew, and robbery sometimes resulted in murder of the victim.

PRISONERS ATTEMPTING TO ESCAPE BY TUNNEL. (NPS)

REBEL MODE OF CAPTURING ESCAPED PRISON-ERS, FROM *LIFE AND DEATH IN REBEL PRISONS*, ROBERT H. KELLOGG, 1866.

(LC)

May 28, 1864

There is one com-modity never had in any market. It is ahead of any Dutch brewery extract; it is meal beer made by let-ting corn meal sour in water. The vender cries, "here is you nice meal beer, right sour, well sea-soned with sas-safras."

John Northup Private, Co. D, 7th Connecticut Inf.

Prisoners wore a star on their hats or some conspicuous place if they were detailed to work. If they were caught out-side the stockade without the star they were taken to Wirz's headquarters to receive what the boys called "the old Captain's jewelry," a 32-pound ball and chain.

As the summer went on it was mush for breakfast, mush for dinner and mush with no salt for supper. The crowding was getting worse and diseases were increas-ing. The rations continued to lessen and many days the prisoners received only a pint of boiled rice with no meat, bread or meal to go with it. The men, with very lit-tle shelter from the weather, were getting sores which in time often turned into gangrene. Diseases and sores were spread through lice. John Ransom wrote that, "Andersonville seems to be headquarters for all the little pests that ever originated, flies by the thousand millions." Lice became as much an enemy as the Confederate guards. Prisoner Bjorn Alakson, Co. H, 9th Minnesota Cavalry

would write, "A man without lice was looked upon as a being to be shunned." Killing lice became a game and would help pass the tedious time.

In regard to some of the problems at the prison Captain Henry Wirz wrote the following letter on June 6th to Captain R.D. Chapman, acting adjutant of post:

CAPTAIN: I most respectfully call the atten-tion of the colonel commanding post through you to the following facts: The bread which is issued to prisoners is of such an inferior quality, consisting fully of one-sixth of husk, that it is almost unfit for use and increases dysentery and other bowel complaints. I would wish that the commis-sary of the post be notified to have the meal bolted or some other contrivance arranged to sift the meal before issuing. If the meal, such as it is now, was sifted the bread

BIRD'S-EYE VIEW OF ANDERSONVILLE PRISON FROM THE SOUTHEAST, LITHOGRAPH BY J. V. MORTON, JR., 1890.

(LC)

rations would fall short fully one-quarter of a pound.

There is a great deficiency of buckets. Rations of rice, beans, vinegar, and molasses cannot be issued to prisoners for want of buckets, at least 8,000 men in the stockade being without anything of the sort. If my information is correct, any number of buckets can be got from Columbus, Georgia, if the quartermaster of the post would make the requisition for the same.

Hoping that you will give us this your attention as soon as possible. I remain, Captain, Most respectfully, your obedient servant.

May 31, 1864

We all expect the lice will rallie on us and take the whole party for a lunch for there isn't enough of us for a meal.

W. F. Lyon Private, Co. C, 9th Minnesota Infantry

Early in the month President Jefferson Davis ordered General John H. Winder to Andersonville as the best qualified officer to command that post. He arrived on June 17, and as soon as he arrived he asked for iron to make baking-pans for the newly constructed bake houses.

By June 17, 21,539 prisoners resided within the 16 1/2 acres surrounded by the stockade walls. By the end of the month there were 25,000, each man having approximately 33 square feet to live on. During the month 7,968 men were admitted to the hospital.

An increase in prisoners meant there were more soldiers who tried to escape. Many tunnels were dug, and some prisoners did get out. Sometimes for a mere morsel of food, prisoners would inform the authorities of escape plans they were aware of, leading to the capture of men. Tunnels were discovered 14 feet deep and from 90 to 100 feet long.

The guards numbered 1,178, many of whom were ill from whooping cough and the measles. Most of the guards were raw recruits. The authorities were always afraid that the prisoners would escape through the tunnels and ravage the surrounding countryside. A letter from General Winder dated June 24, 1864, echoed the need for more guards: "Twenty five thousand men, by the mere force of numbers, can accomplish a great deal. If successful, the result to

LIVING CONDITIONS AT ANDERSONVILLE
portrayed by NPS VOLUNTEERS.

(NPS)

CAMP MORTON

Camp Morton was located in Indianapolis, Indiana. The first prisoners arrived on February 22, 1862. The camp closed in July, 1865. The camp had run-down barracks and the hospital facilities were inadequate. The prisoners did not have enough blankets or clothing. Rations were sparse. During its existence, it was reported that Camp Morton held 12,082 prisoners and 1,763, or 14.6%, died.

The dead were buried at Greenlawn Cemetery. Some were taken south by relatives after the war. The bodies were later moved to Section 32 of Crown Hill Cemetery in Indianapolis. The location is marked by a stone monument.

(UNIVERSITY OF GEORGIA)

May 28, 1864

A man named Turner, who lived near the prison kept a pack of bloodhounds, and he was employed by Capt. Wirz to catch those who escaped. Every morning at daylight the dogs were called together, and with their master, who was mounted on a large bay horse, they made a circuit of the prison.

Josiah Brownell Private, Co. A, 13th U.S. Infantry

the country would be much more disastrous than a defeat of the armies; it would result in the total ruin and devastation of this whole section of the country. Every house would be burned, violence to women, destruction of crops, carrying off negroes, horses, mules, and wagons. It is impossible to estimate the extent of such a disaster. A little timely, prudent preparation will easily render it impossible." At the bottom of this letter, he wrote, "We have just discovered a tunnel reaching 130 feet outside the stockade." On June 20 it was reported that two guards had been hanged for attempting to escape with the prisoners.

While the month of June found the prison authorities pleading for more guards, the doctors desperately sought more tents and supplies. The new hospital on the outside of the prison had tents for 800, and there were 1,035 in the hospital with another 3,000 sick in the compound. As Private Aslaksan, 9th Minnesota Cavalry, later wrote, "The sight of all this misery, the starved, dying and half-naked humans all around,

those with scurvy misshaped limbs, swollen limbs, swollen joints, and festering sores infected with gangrene, all contributed to make the newcomer so unnerved that he would soon get into a mental condition of dispair out of which the ghost beacon of death seemed welcome."

A select group of 300 prisoners worked on the outside of the stockade. They went into the country to get vegetables and perform odd jobs. They had a camp of their own with only one officer to guard them. They chopped logs for the stockade addition, worked in the bakery where provisions for the prisoners in the stockade were cooked, and worked as carpenters. They also buried the dead and served as teamsters and litter-bearers.

It was the end of June when, with the help of Captain Wirz, the "Raiders" were identified and removed from the stockade for trial. Throughout the existence of the camp these men had robbed, murdered and in all ways made life even more horrible for the prisoners. A police force

June 1, 1864

Took a walk around camp. Deplorable sight. Some without clothing, some in last agonies of death; others writhing under the pangs of disease or wounds; some as black as mulattos with smoke and dirt.

Eugene Forbes Sgt., Co. B, 4th New Jersey Infantry

had been organized within the prison called "The Regulators" which was headed up by a man known as "Limber Jim."

On June 30, under the signature of General Winder, it was determined that the Raiders would be tried for crimes against their fellow prisoners. Winder said in his order, "On such trials the charges will be distinctly made with specifications setting forth time and place, a copy of which will be furnished the accused. The proceedings, findings, and sentence in each case will be sent to the commanding officer for record, and if found in order and proper, the sentence will be ordered for execution."

The trial was held and some of the guilty Raiders were ordered to wear a ball and chain, while others were strung up by their thumbs or set in the stocks. Six of the leaders: Collins, Delaney, Curtis, Rickson, Sarsfield and Munn, were found guilty of murder and were ordered to be hanged. Their sentence was to be carried out the following month.

On July 11, 1864, the six Raider leaders were hanged. During the execution

attempt Collins' rope broke and he tried to escape. He was caught by fellow prisoners and was hanged for a second time, begging for his life.

On July 1 the addition to the prison had been completed, adding another ten acres to the stockade. It was now 26 1/2 acres. There were 26,367 prisoners in the compound. At 10:00 in the morning the moving commenced and it continued until

A CAMP SCENE

(NPS)

sundown. At least 10,000 prisoners crowded through an opening. Of the 90 detachments in the prison, 45 detachments were ordered to move. There was a stampede for the new ground and many of the prisoners were hurt pressing through the 12-foot opening. The crowd was so great that the sick, falling down in the press, were trampled and killed; strong men became wedged between the moving mass and the standing timbers. How many were killed outright is not known. A large number of strong and weak alike were so injured that they never recovered.

From the July 1 *Sumter Republican:* "Andersonville Prison Camp (called Camp

Sumter in this story) has been enlarged. It is now 20 acres sufficient for...50,000 of Linkhorn's hirelings. There are 27,000 there now and 500 to 1000 a day...make applications for admittance. The mortality is about fifty a day." Actually during the month of July, 1,817 died—nearly 59 a day.

Those who had gone to the new side of the prison found that the clay in the ground was suitable for the making of brick or adobe by mixing it with water. Scores of prisoners thus went into the brickmaking business. A great many of them built the walls of their huts with this adobe mixture, which hardened nicely in the Georgia sun.

When the new portion of the prison was opened, the inmates took the wood from the old wall and used it for their shebangs and for cooking raw rations. This so infuriated Captain Wirz that they did not get rations for two days. According to Private John Northrup, 7th Connecticut Infantry, Captain Wirz was heard to say that "he would learn the God damn Yankees that he was in command and if the sons of bitches died like hell there would be enough left." After the prisoners had been without rations for two days, the authorities distributed beef. After being held for over two days the beef was crawling with vermin when finally served, but the famished men dared not allow such trifles to stand in the way of satisfying their hunger, and it was devoured with a relish.

Bread was baked in the prison ovens and was devoured by the prisoners.

June 11, 1864

I went down to the gate and got the exact number of prisoners in the bull pen both black and white and I found them to be 22,330 and we are all packed on ten acre square. There is 18 in the piece but 8 of it is taken up for what is called the dead line and woe to the yank that gets his body inside of that line for every yank they shoot they get 30 days furlough and they don't stop to let you get in far before rip goes you jacket.

Albert H. Schatzel

June 17, 1864

It was often that the last to arrive at the prison were the first to succumb. The beans were so wormy and weavel eaten that it took one of us to skim off the maggots and insects all the time it was boiling.

Bjorn Aslaksan Pvt., Co. H, 9th Minnesota Cavalry

Captain Wirz, at the recommendation of the medical staff, began the brewing of "corn beer." This was given to those suffering from scurvy and acted as an antidote to the scorbutic poison. The beer was made from cornmeal and whole corn scalded in hot water until it turned to mash. Some yeast was added to promote fermentation, and in a few days a sharp acid beverage was produced which was very wholesome and palatable. As prisoner John E. Warren, 7th Wisconsin Artillery wrote, "This same corn beer was made within the stockade by the prisoners, but not to the extent that it was manufactured on the outside, nor of so good a quality." The food situation seemed to be improving since prisoners could also buy green corn within the stockade at 25 cents per ear.

Food, water and death were on the minds of all of the prisoners. Prisoner Asa B. Isham, Co. F, 7th Michigan Cavalry, would write in later years, "A few steps to the right we find a hideous object lying in a hole, which his hands have scooped out in the sand. The tattered rags that partially cover him can not conceal the bones that gleam through the skin; his eyes move fearfully in his head, his hands clench tightly together, his limbs are drawn up in horrible contortions by the cramp. Placing our ear to his lips, we gather from his faint whispers that but a short time before he had left a happy home, flushed with hope and courage, to battle for liberty and right. A fond mother pressed her lips to his brow as, with tearful eyes, she bade him farewell; in the field he had performed deeds of valor. He was captured, and even while we linger beside him a faint shudder passes through his frame, and all is over."

Money and wordly goods could keep a man alive, especially during the difficult days of the summer of 1864. Captain Wirz had allowed sutlers inside the walls to sell items to the prisoners. If a prisoner had money, and many did, he could buy the necessities of life: peas, pones, wheat, flour and salt. These items were very expensive and rapidly ate up the prisoner's money. Luxuries such as tobacco, onions, eggs, soda, red pepper, gingerbread, soap, taffy, sour beer, apples and peaches were available to those with money. A great variety of items were exchanged for food: money, gold and silver watches and rings, shrewdly

CAMP LAWTON

Camp Lawton was located about five miles from Millen, Georgia, and on the Augusta Railroad. The prison was laid out in the customary style of Confederate prisons with sloping hills at each end and a small stream flowing between the hills. The walls were 15 feet high and sufficient wood was left inside the walls so that the prisoners could construct crude huts. Rations were somewhat better than Andersonville but were still not sufficient to sustain life.

The prison was open for two months. The Lawton cemetery held 784 bodies. These bodies were moved to Beaufort National Cemetery in South Carolina in February 1868. Where Camp Lawton stood in 1868 there is now a state park, Magnolia Springs.

(GEORGIA DEPT. OF NATURAL RESOURCES)

secreted from the sharp-eyed officials during the search prior to admission to the prison. Other valuable items included pocket-knives, mugs carved from wood and laurel pipe bowls. These could be easily traded with the guards. A peach could be purchased for fifty cents; salt, twenty-five cents per tablespoon; and soap, one dollar and a half per bar. The traders were noisy and persistent when yelling their wares: "Who has this nice ration of beef, for ten cents, only ten cents." "Here you can buy your cheap onions, only seventy-five cents apiece." Money or worldly goods could keep a man alive, mostly during the difficult days of the summer of 1864.

John Warren, 7th Wisconsin Artillery, later wrote of an encounter with Captain Wirz on July 16, 1864. "I met Wirz while on one of his inside visits. He stopped his horse, and I explained to him briefly the situation and the condition of my comrades. Said I, 'if something is not to be done for them at once, in a few days death will be the result'; and this was the substance of his reply, 'I am doing all I can, I am hampered and pressed for rations. I am even exceeding my authority

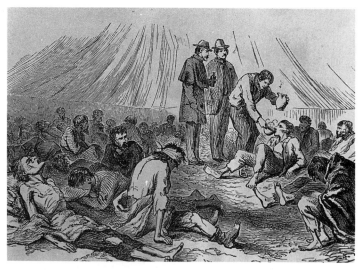

JOHNSON'S ISLAND

Johnson's Island is located three miles north of Sandusky, Ohio, in Sandusky Bay. The island consists of 300 acres of clay and loam soil, two to eight feet deep, underneath which is solid limestone. The prison was located in a cleared area of fifteen acres on the southeast shore of the island. The area was surrounded by a plank stockade fourteen feet high. The prisoner's quarters were comprised of thirteen two-story barrack type frame buildings. Each building was 120 feet by 28 feet, designed to accommodate 250 men. There was a woodburning stove in each building. Water was obtained from two surface wells, but pipes were installed later from the bay.

The first prisoners arrived in April 1862. The prison was an officer's prison. Over the period of 40 months the prison was open, at least 12,000 Confederate officers were imprisoned at Johnson's Island. All that remains today of Johnson's Island prison is the cemetery where 206 Confederate soldiers and a few enlisted men are buried. At the entrance to the cemetery stands a statue of a Confederate soldier peering out over the waters of the bay. It is called "The Outlook."

(MC)

June 23, 1864

Another pass time was whitteling. Give a Yankee a jack knife and he can make almost anything. The rebels found out the most expert whittlers and furnished them materials to work upon and thus many prisoners earned extra rations in this way.

Thomas A. Gossett Private, Co. I, 7th Indiana Infantry

in issuing supplies. I am blamed by the prisoners for all of this suffering. They do not or will not realize that I am a subordinate, governed by orders of my commanding officer. Why, sir, my own men are on short rations. The best I can do is to see that your sick comrades are removed to the hospital. God help you, I cannot, and his eyes were filled with tears."

On July 18 in a letter to Richmond, General Winder begged for $100,000 for the prisoners and $75,000 for pay of the officers and men of the guard. On July 21 he reported that there were now 29,201 prisoners in the stockade including 1,735 in the hospital. He reported that he had a complement of 2,421 guards with 517 on sick call each day.

It was in the latter part of July that a petition was circulated throughout the prison that was to be taken to the proper authorities in Washington, D.C., describing the atrocious living conditions of the prisoners. John Warren, 7th Wisconsin Artillery, wrote that the document declared, "We earnestly yet respectfully pray that some

CARRYING OUT THE DEAD, NPS VOLUNTEER LIVING HISTORY PROGRAM.

(NPS)

24

action be taken immediately to effect our speedy release, either on parole or by exchange, the dictates of both humanity and justice alike demanding it on the part of our Government. We shall look forward with a hopeful confidence that something will be done speedily in this matter, believing that a proper statement of the facts is all that is necessary to secure a redress of the grievance complained of." Although this petition was taken to Washington by prisoners on August 4, nothing ever came of it.

There were many church meetings among the prisoners with Boston Corbett, among others, doing the ministering. There were reports of two Catholic priests, including Father Peter Whelan, working among the prisoners. As Reverend H. Claverevel wrote, "The religious work among the prisoners found expression in the throngs of individuals we met here and there, bowed down in the attitude of prayer or listening to a comrade who was reading from the Bible or addressing to them words of exhortation."

During July Confederate officials at Andersonville had plenty of reasons for concern. General William T. Sherman's army was near Atlanta and prison officials feared he would head toward Andersonville. They were also concerned that the prisoners, fueled by reports of new arrivals, would attempt a mass uprising. During this time slaves from surrounding farms were brought in to fell trees and dig additional earthworks in anticipation of a cavalry attack.

The concern was not unfounded. General Sherman did order two cavalry units to ride south and cut the Macon railroad. He also granted permission to General George Stoneman, who

commanded one of these units, to advance on Macon itself. Stoneman planned to free the Union officers at Camp Oglethorpe in Macon, then make his way south to free the 29,000 prisoners at Andersonville.

General Stoneman had 2,500 men and a two-gun battery. At 3:00 a.m. on July 27, he left Atlanta and rode south. Before noon on the 29th the Union cavalry reached Clinton, but the Confederates were following them with 4,000 cavalry. Stoneman met the Georgia militia, and in a number of skirmishes Stoneman's cavalry was defeated. The Union cavalry members were either killed or taken prisoner. The Confederates captured about 500 prisoners and took them to Andersonville. The prison's teeming population had been increased, not freed. During this period, a total of 1,200

prisoners was added to the population by the last day of July.

It was now August and during the month 2,933 would die. There were 1,305 sick in the hospital and 5,100 ill in the stockade. The average number of men in the stockade during August was 32,899,

HANGING OF THE RAIDERS IN ANDERSONVILLE PRISON FROM BATTLEFIELD AND PRISON PEN.

The common shelter was constructed with blankets, old shirts, half shelters tents, etc., some burrowed into the ground, while others had no shelter at all.

Warren Goss

July 2, 1864

Early in the morning seen a boy about to die. The little fellow called for his mother.

Albert H. Schatzel

Richmond pleading for badly needed medicine, food, tents, tools and lumber, to no avail. As Private Northrup, 7th Connecticut Infantry, wrote, "One poor boy near cried all night and wished to die and suffer no longer; he is an awful object; his clothing is gone but a rag of a shirt; his body is a mere frame; his hair has fallen out from his head; his scurvy ankles and feet are as large as his waist. I never saw a sight more appalling. Than the awful thought that he is a man, somebody's darling boy, dead, and yet breathing." And so it went.

each having less than six square feet to call his own. In a letter to Colonel Chandler on August 1, Captain Wirz wrote, "As long as 30,000 men are confined in any one enclosure the proper policing is altogether impossible. A long confinement had

LOOKING SOUTH FROM THE SINKS, ANDERSONVILLE PRISON, AUGUST 1864. NOTE THE SINKS, THE SHEBANGS, STOCKADE, AND THE PIGEON ROOSTS.

(LC)

depressed the spirits of thousands, and they are utterly indifferent. Hoping your official report will make such an impression with the authorities at Richmond that they will issue the necessary orders to enable us to get what we so badly need."

The chief surgeon at the post and Captain Wirz kept directing letters to

The prisoners were dying at a rate of 100 per day. When a man died a label was attached to his body, giving his name and regiment. He was then taken to the Dead

Cahaba Prison

Cahaba Prison was located in Cahaba, Alabama, approximately ten miles south of Selma at the junction of the Cahaba and Alabama Rivers. It was established in the summer of 1863. It was closed six to nine months later and the prisoners were sent to Andersonville. It was reestablished the last six months of the war. The prison was originally a warehouse. It became so crowded each man barely had enough room to lie down. Wooden bunks without straw or bedding slept 432 men. Water came from a natural spring which ran through the prison and emptied into the river. This spring was also used as the sinks.

Cahaba Prison held about 5,000 men altogether and was probably the best run of all Southern prisons. It is hard to say how many prisoners died at Cahaba. Confederate records list 142, while Federal records show 147. The dead were buried at a nearby cemetery and after the war the graves were dug up and the bodies were reburied at Marietta, Georgia.

July 4, 1864

So far as I know, the idea that brought about the overthrow of the murderous raiders came from Wirz himself; and it is certain that the efforts of the "law and order" organization, and of the police force, all of whom deserve great credit in arresting the "raiders", would have been fruitless but for the cooperation of Wirz.

John E. Warren, Wisconsin Artillery

House, or more properly dead yard. The Dead House was located opposite the South Gate. When a person died he was buried naked, since the clothes were needed by the living prisoners both to wear and to build shebangs. Each day the dead were delivered to the graveyard in a lumber wagon. Twenty bodies constituted a load. The corpses were carried in full sight of the stockade, piled like pork, with limbs sticking out of the wagon.

By August 4 there were 33,000 prisoners inside the stockade including the 2,208 who were in the hospital. It was on the 5th of the month that a report was made to Richmond by the inspector general in which he wrote, "My duty requires me respectfully to recommend a change in the officer in command of this post, Brigadier General J.H. Winder, and the substitution in his place of some one who unites both energy and good judgement with some feelings of humanity and consideration for the welfare and comfort of the vast

THE BAKERY CONTAINED TWO ROOMS, ONE OF WHICH HAD TWO OVENS. THESE TWO OVENS, FOURTEEN FEET IN LENGTH BY SEVEN FEET IN WIDTH, SUPPLIED THE PRISONERS WITH BREAD.

(LC)

July 16, 1864

*Today a tunnel
was discovered by
the rebel authori-
ties. 4 of the pris-
oners had dug a
well 60 feet deep
about 20 feet
down they had
struck out dug 20
feet out side the
stockade and were
a going to escape
in 10 nights, one
of our men
betrayed them
for a plug
of tobacco.*

*Samuel Burdick
Private, Co. H,
17th Iowa Infantry*

number of unfortunates placed under his control; some one who at least will not advocate deliberately and in cold blood the propriety of leaving them in their present condition until their number has been sufficiently reduced by death to make the present arrangements suffice for their accommodation, and who will not consider it a matter of self-laudation and boasting that he has been inside the stockade, a place of horrors of which it is difficult to describe, and which is a disgrace to civilization."

The prisoners dug holes, not only for escape but for water. Some just dug holes to get out of the Georgia heat. The northern prisoners suffered in the heat of the South while the southern men suffered from the northern cold. Many of the holes would cave in and the prisoner would be suffocated. (At the turn of the century a storm revealed two bodies buried beneath the stockade site.) The water holes were drying up in the hot summer months of July and August, and the prisoners were praying for water in

A 19TH CENTURY LITHOGRAPH DRAWN FROM THE MEMORY OF PRISONER THOMAS O'DEA.

(NPS)

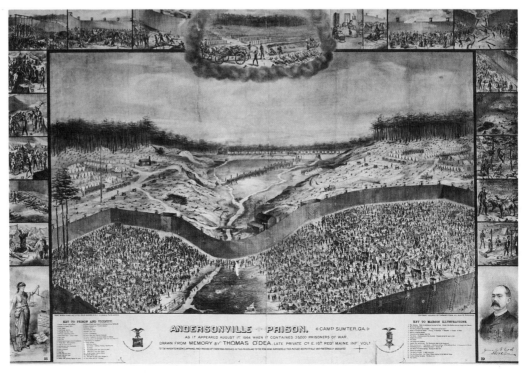

DORENCE ATWATER

For prisoners who died at Camp Sumter, record keeping was shabby at best. There was great concern that after the war relatives would not be able to locate and identify the bodies of their loved ones. Into this situation stepped one prisoner, Dorence Atwater, of the 2nd New York Cavalry. Sent to Andersonville, Atwater was detailed as a clerk to the surgeon who recorded all the daily deaths. Secretly, Atwater compiled a duplicate list of names and regiments of the deceased, keying them to numbers that were inscribed on the hastily erected posts or boards that were placed over the graves. With the war over, Atwater eventually saw this list of 12,912 names published, thereby enabling proper identification of the graves. He received no reward for his efforts, but Dorence Atwater was a true hero of the Civil War.

earnest. On the night of August 9 there was a heavy rain. It swelled the stream to a river and tore down the stockade where the stream ran into and out of the prison. Two cannon shots rang out from Star Fort and many of the sentinels fired at the prisoners thinking they would make a break out of the stockade. Some prisoners plunged into the flood to bring out floating timber or pieces of boards that had come down. The guards stood in line of battle for more than an hour, and when the rain ceased, they only had time to temporarily repair the damage before night. The storm had cleaned out "Stockade Branch" and the entire swamp inside the prison. As W.F. Lyon, Company C, 9th Minnesota Infantry, put it, "When the almighty cleans house he puts housekeepers to shame." The storm had created a stream of water inside the deadline just below the north gate. An ingenious Yank managed to get part of a sapling and used it to form a trough that reached from the outside of the deadline to the spring. With this trough he led the water like an old-fashioned eaves trough. The prisoners now had access to the spring water. The stream was named "Providence Spring."

Prison authorities began repairing the old wall where the stream crossed it and they also began building a second wall outside the original wall. The new wall was erected to help stem the building of tunnels and for better security. During the first part of August, General Winder made a report to the inspector general regarding a new prison to be built at Millen, Georgia. "I do beg that you will give the officer at Millen full authority to press everything, including land, houses, teams, wagons, saw-mills, to enable him to press the work forward, so that we may relieve this prison." He also reported, "Colonel Forno (officer over the guards) is quite sick, Captain is very sick, produced entirely

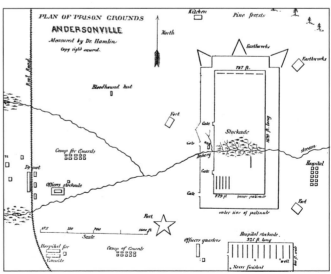

PLAN OF PRISON GROUNDS DRAWN IN 1865 BY DR. HAMLIN.

by overwork for want of assistance. He ought to have gone to bed two weeks ago, but kept up because he had none to whom the command could be turned over."

Beef was sometimes issued at Andersonville, and it was said that it was always stale and could be smelled at a great distance. Prisoners who had been captive for some time did not seem to mind the smell and only thought of quantity, but new arrivals found the smell nauseating. Beef bones, without meat, were sold inside the stockade at twenty-five cents a piece and always had to undergo a pounding process to extract the rich oil they contained. After the pounding they were used in soup.

Among the greatest scourges at Andersonville were the lice, flies and maggots. They were in the prisoners' clothes, on their bodies, in their shebangs, in the sand and in the food. Charles C. Fosdick, 5th Iowa Infantry, complained that, "Thus, night and day for dreary weeks, lengthening into

long months, we were continually annoyed by the lice, maggots, flies and mosquitoes until our aggravations in this respect became almost beyond endurance."

The prisoners died in their shebangs, in the hospital, and in the swamp. A man could go to sleep at night and find two of his tent-mates dead in the morning. Some expired so quietly that it would have been impossible to determine when their last breath was drawn.

On August 17, 1864, a Confederate photographer, A.J. Riddle, arrived at the prison. Many of the prisoners commented

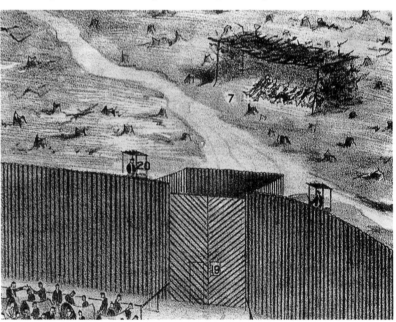

ILLUSTRATION BY THOMAS O'DEA OF THE "DEAD HOUSE" (TOP RIGHT).

(NPS)

ILLUSTRATION FROM *LIFE AND DEATH IN REBEL PRISONS* SHOWS THE FLOOD CAUSING PART OF THE STOCKADE TO COLLAPSE.

on him in later years. He took photographs from sentry boxes at different points around the stockade.

Late in August Captain Winder wrote to the quartermaster in Macon that work at the stockade had ceased for the lack of nails. According to Winder, he needed 200 kegs of nails with 100 kegs being 8-penny and the rest assorted. In addition he asked for leather, 250 tents, a blacksmith's bellows and shipment of iron and steel. He also asked for iron kettles for the cookhouse.

On August 21 Union General Ulysses Grant wrote Secretary of War Edwin M. Stanton, "Please inform General Foster that under no circumstances will he be authorized to make an exchange of prisoners of war. Exchanges simply reinforce the enemy

THIS PHOTOGRAPH TAKEN IN 1897 SHOWS FORMER PRISONERS WHO RETURNED TO ANDERSONVILLE TO DRINK WATER FROM PROVIDENCE SPRING.

(LC)

August 9, 1864

On the 7th, 8th, and 9th the weather was so awfully hot that it really appeared as if the heat would kill us all; those were the most terrible days in the history of our prison. On the 9th one hundred and seventy five prisoners died, and the mortality in the three days was nearly five hundred.

John W. Urban

at once, whilst we do not get the benefit for two or three months, and lose the majority entirely."

The pall of death that hung over the 26 1/2 acres in August was stronger than any other month that the prison was in operation. The gravediggers were kept busy and listing of the names of the dead by a New York Cavalry Sergeant, Dorence Atwater, became a 24-hour job. As Melvin Grisby, Co. F, 23rd Kentucky Infantry, wrote in his diary in August, "I bought a chance to go out with a dead body. I had to carry the end of the stretcher on which the head lay. The stretcher was an old gunny-sack nailed to poles. The sack part was too short. The feet hung over it at one end and the head at the

other. There had been no tender loving hand to close those eyes when the last breath had gone. They were open and glaring. The head hung over my end of the stretcher and the eyes glared up at me. They haunted me for weeks. I never bought another corpse."

Rumors, or "war-chin" as the prisoners called them, never stopped. The rumors spread like wildfire through camp: "Sherman is falling back in front of Atlanta;" "Sherman fell back on the left, drawing Hood after him, then threw in his right wing and captured 22,000;" "Parole has been agreed to by the Commissioners of both the Confederates and Yankees." These rumors kept some men alive by providing hope of imminent release.

After six months the authorities showed some form of organization with the "Rules of Andersonville Prison." John Warren, 7th Wisconsin Artillery, recalled that there were thirteen rules including, "There will be two daily roll calls at the prison, one at 8 a.m. and one at 4 p.m.," and "To prevent stealing in camp the prisoners have the right to elect a chief of police who will select as many men as he

THIS 1867 PHOTOGRAPH SHOWS THE INNER AND MIDDLE STOCKADES, WEST FRONTS, LOOKING SOUTH.

(NA)

ROCK ISLAND PRISON

*R*ock Island Prison was located on a government-owned island between Davenport, Iowa, and Moline, Illinois. For the past century it was known as Rock Island Arsenal. The prison camp was constructed in mid-1863 and received its first prisoners that December. The prison camp was comprised of 84 prisoner barracks, each being 100 feet long, 22 feet wide and 12 feet high. A kitchen was built into each barracks. They had 60 double bunks, and each building could house 120 prisoners. Also, over a period of time other buildings were erected: a laundry, guardhouse, dead house and dispensary.

The barracks were enclosed by a stockade fence 1,300 feet long, 900 feet wide, and 12 feet high. A boardwalk was constructed on the outside of the fence, and sentry boxes were placed every 100 feet.

During the 20 months the prison was open, 1,960 prisoners died and 171 Union guards died. The Confederate cemetery was located 1,000 yards southeast of the prison stockade. Prison guards were buried on a site about 100 yards northwest of the Confederate cemetery.

deems necessary to assist him. He and his sergeants of the divisions have a right to punish any man who is detected stealing. The punishment shall be shaving of one half of the head and a number of lashes, not exceeding fifty." The rules were long overdue in the running of the prison.

The framework of the barracks was completed in September. There were four barracks that housed 270 prisoners each. When the men started moving in, two more barracks were nearing completion. They were near the north end in the new section of the prison. During September 2,677 prisoners died. Between the end of

February, when the prison was established, and September 21, a total of 9,479 prisoners had died, or 23.3 percent of those who had been confined at Andersonville. The death register listed the greatest killer as diarrhea (3,530 deaths) and dysentery (999 deaths). The two together accounted for 58.7 percent of the deaths during the first six months.

Starting in September, some of the healthier prisoners were moved in detachments from Andersonville to Camp Lawton at Millen, Georgia, and to Florence, South Carolina. The prisoners were moved not only because of overcrowded conditions

August 12, 1864

We had a chance to look around and see what the storm had done for us. The entire prison, including the swamp, was swept in such a manner as to be quite clean compared to its former condition. Almost all the filth and vermon on the ground was swept away. It was soon discovered that a strong, pure spring of water had burst out. The water was cool and pure in great contrast to the filthy stuff we had been using.

John W. Urban

FATHER WHELAN

Father Peter Whelan was born in 1802 in County Wexford, Ireland and migrated to America while still a young man. He became a priest in the Catholic Church and spent 19 years at a church in Locust Grove, Georgia. Early in the Civil War his ministry took him to Fort Pulaski to minister to the Confederate troops. He was taken prisoner when Fort Pulaski fell but after a short time was paroled. Father Whelan heard of Andersonville and the privation that existed there. With the sanction of the church he made the trip to Andersonville and arrived on June 16, 1864. He stayed until October, ministering to the prisoners at the risk of his own health. He borrowed $16,000 in Confederate money and in January 1865 went to Americus and bought ten thousand pounds of wheat flour. Baked into bread and distributed at the prison hospital, it lasted several months. This became known as "Whelan's Bread." One prisoner said afterward, "Without doubt he was the means of saving hundreds of lives."

but also due to the movement of Sherman's army near Atlanta. Some men believed they were part of a general exchange of prisoners. S.M. Dufur, Co. B, 1st Vermont Cavalry wrote, "We said it cannot be any worse if we are even going to another prison, it will be change." By September 8, five thousand or more had left. With the exodus of so many prisoners the sick and dying became more obvious to the bystander.

Sick prisoners who could not get into the hospital were moved into the new barracks, which were only slightly more comfortable than a hovel in the ground. Henry Milton Roach, Co. G, 78 Ohio Infantry, wrote, "One of the most pitiful scenes that came before any observation was that of a man of middle age, who through patriotism, had sacrificed the dearest ties to man, that of leaving wife and children, all that his country and flag might live. This man became insane and believed he was at home with his family, describing all of the circumstances of his home life. This poor victim whom I have described was finally released by death, but the last lingering word from his lips was "Mary."

Some of the parolees' duty outside the prison was to bury the dead. They dug trenches about one hundred and sixty feet long and three feet deep with a one foot deep vault at the bottom. They split slabs of wood and placed them over each of the dead. James R. Compton, Co. F, 4th Iowa Infantry, wrote, "It is no small task to bury one hundred and twenty men each day. So badly would they decompose during the interval between death and burial that often we found, when we attempted to lift them, that the skin slipped from the flesh, and often the flesh cleared from the bone.

WHEN A.J. RIDDLE TOOK THIS PHOTOGRAPH ON AUGUST 17, 1864, THERE WERE ALMOST 33,000 PRISONERS CONFINED WITHIN ANDERSONVILLE'S 26 1/2 ACRES.

(LC)

Here comes a government wagon piled full of our brave boys; thrown into the wagon like a lot of dead swine, to be rudely thrown out again on their arrival at the burial ground."

It was the end of September and the stockade that had held over 30,000 a few weeks earlier was nearly empty. Only those who could not walk remained, besides the prisoners who had to work on the outside of the prison to keep it operating.

Those who did remain continued to find ways to occupy their time. As William B. Clifton, Co. K, 37th Indiana Cavalry, wrote, "Well, we had to have some kind of amusement and so they had lice races. They could get a tin plate and make a small ring in the center of the plate, heat it in the sun, drop two lice on the center of the plate, and bet on the one getting out of the ring first. One person would say, 'drop' and the lice were dropped on the plate and the lice would start to run to get off of the hot plate. I seen poor

fellows crawl up to look at the lice race that would be dead in thirty minutes."

In a letter dated September 29, 1864, Major General H.W. Hallux, chief of staff of the Union Armies, wrote J.G. Foster, who was in charge of exchange of prisoners at Hilton Head, South Carolina. In the letter Hallux stated, "Hereafter no exchange of prisoners shall be entertained except on the field when captured. Every attempt at special or general exchange has been met by the enemy with bad faith. It is understood that arrangements may be made later toward exchange of sick and disabled men on each side."

By the first of October, Andersonville ceased to be a receiving depot for prisoners. Only those who could not travel were left. It became a prison hospital. But with such a high proportion of the prisoners left

August 13, 1864

Occupying a wall-tent near our dispensary was a lady with a young child. I at first supposed that she was the wife of one of the officers in charge, but soon learned that she was a prisoner, having been captured in company with her husband, who was steamboat captain and a civilian.

*Solon Hyde
Private, 17th
Ohio Infantry*

POINT LOOKOUT PRISON

oint Lookout Prison was located at the extreme tip of St. Mary's County, Maryland, at the confluence of the Chesapeake Bay and the Potomac River. The size of the camp was 1,000 feet square, about 23 acres, surrounded by a board fence 12 feet high with a platform on the outside for the guards. The prisoners were housed in tents. The tents were arranged on nine streets or divisions running east and west. The prison was opened July 1863 and closed June 1865. Twenty thousand, one hundred and ten prisoners went through the facility during its existence, and 3,389, or 17%, died. The deaths came from bad management, lack of adequate supplies such as clothing, blankets, wood and food, failure to establish sanitary conditions, and brutality and senseless killing by the guards.

(NA)

being sick the mortality rate rose dramatically. Besides the 8,218 prisoners present on October 1, another 444 were added during the month. Of those 8,662 men, 3,913 received treatment in the hospital and of these 1,560 died. Twenty eight escaped and 2,811 were transferred to other prisons.

It was reported by the surgeon in charge, R.R. Stevenson, that with the overcrowding of the prison now over, the incidence of mortality at the post was decreasing and that a careful analysis of the soil and water proved that Andersonville was one of the healthiest places in the Confederacy. He also reported that they were building sheds and other suitable hospital buildings and in the course of one month ample accommodations would be made for 2,000 patients at Andersonville. He called attention to the importance of preventing the crowding of prisoners at any other post.

The prisoners now had a roll call every morning and were formed into detachments

NPS VOLUNTEERS PORTRAYING CAMP LIVING CONDITIONS.

(NPS)

of 500 each. There were approximately 2,500 healthy men and 1,280 sick. The rations now included bread baked in cakes or loaves about two feet square and four inches thick. The prisoners received soup in boots, bootleg buckets, and drawer and pantaloons legs secured at the bottom. Although the food had improved somewhat and the crowding was over, the death rate was still high.

In November 499 died. There were 1,359 prisoners on hand. Captain Wirz complained about prisoners escaping every night because he did not have enough guards.

According to the Sanitary Commission in the North, from July to November 1864 they sent to Andersonville 5,000 sheets, 7,000 pairs of drawers, 4,000 handkerchiefs, 600 overcoats, blankets, shoes, canned milk, coffee, farina, cornstarch and tobacco in corresponding quantities. This could not overcome the effects of over-

crowding, the stinking swamp nor the lack of shelter and medicine.

It was the beginning of winter and the guards relaxed much of their sternness and rigor. The prisoners entered into conversation with them, and trading became more prevalent. The prisoners made toothpicks out of bones from the meat they were fed. They made pipes out of green

LEAVING ANDERSONVILLE, ANDERSONVILLE MILITARY PRISON SERIES BY J.E. TAYLOR, 1898.

(LC)

PRISON GUARDS AT ANDERSONVILLE

September 1, 1864

During most of the prison's existence the Georgia Reserve comprised the guard. Most of them were young boys or old men. During the 14 months of the prison's existance, over 200 of them died. Most of these (117) were buried nearby. When the cemetery wall was erected in 1878, the guard cemetery was left outside the wall. The United Daughters of the Confederacy, which had been saving money for a monument, used the funds to have the bodies disinterred and moved to Oak Grove Cemetery in Americus.

(NPS LIVING HISTORY PROGRAM)

From the fourth of July until the first day of September, every day in those two months, I killed three hundred lice and nits. When I got up to this number I would stop killing until the next day.

Edmund J. Gibson Pvt., Co. K, 25th Maryland Inf.

CAMP OGLETHORPE

September 13,
1864

*On the 13th of
September the
only remaining
one of my compa-
ny died, leaving
me alone as far as
my company was
concerned. This
event made me
very sad. I, the
youngest boy in
the regiment, and
sick besides, I
nerved up for the
worst and
resolved to stand
the thing through,
that I might tell
the poor boys'
friends where they
died.*

Charles Fosdick

Camp Oglethorpe Prison was located near Macon, Georgia. It was used to confine Union military officers during the last full year of the Civil War, 1864. The officers survived well. No ill-treatment was noted by the over 1,600 officers confined at Macon. Only one officer was shot and killed by a Confederate sentinel for crossing the deadline. The camp was located south of Macon on a sandy incline formerly used as the county fairgrounds. Shelter was provided for the Union prisoners as well as water and wood for heating. The old Floral Hall, a one-story frame building located in the center of the fairground, was used to house 200 men. A stockade 16 feet high and similar in construction to the Andersonville stockade, surrounded the enclosure.

A raid on Macon in late July by General George Stoneman's cavalry persuaded Confederate authorities to remove prisoners from Macon to Charleston and Savannah. By the end of September 1864 the prison virtually ceased operation.

wood that they picked up while outside the stockade. Prices for the items depended on the amount of time a prisoner put into his pipe or toothpick. Another business opportunity was called "raising" in which the amount of a Confederate note was increased. The script was poorly made, both in design and execution. The

PRISONERS ENTERING ANDERSONVILLE PRISON ILLUSTRATION FROM *BATTLEFIELD AND PRISON PEN*.

ELMIRA PRISON

Elmira, New York, is situated five miles from the Pennsylvania line. In the beginning the camp was used for new recruits, but by May 15, 1864, some of the barracks were set aside for prisoners-of-war. A twelve-foot-high fence was constructed, framed on the outside with a sentry's walk four feet below the top and built at a safe distance from the barracks. Housing consisted of thirty-five two-story barracks each measuring 100 by 20 feet. Two rows of bunks were along the walls and as the prison became crowded some prisoners lived in "A" tents.

The first group of prisoners, shipped from Point Lookout, Maryland, arrived at Elmira on July 6 and numbered 399 men. By the end of July, 4,424 prisoners were packed in the compound with another 3,000 en route. By mid-August the number leaped to 9,600. The inmates of Elmira weathered hunger, illness and melancholia but, even worse, exposure to the elements. Late in the winter of 1864-65 some stoves were distributed to the prisoners but not enough for everyone. The southerners were exposed to temperatures of ten to fifteen degrees below zero and many succumbed to freezing.

Of the total of 12,123 soldiers imprisoned at Elmira, 2,963 died of sickness, exposure and associated causes. The camp was officially closed on July 5, 1865. All that remains today of Elmira Prison is a well-kept cemetery along the banks of the Chemung River.

(LC)

prisoners always tried to get change in "ones" or "twos." The $1 bill would be converted into a $10 bill and the $2 bill would be made into a $20 bill. The counterfeiter guaranteed his work and style of art to his customers.

On November 8 the prisoners held an election for President. Four thousand six hundred votes were cast. Lincoln secured a 734 majority. The prisoners hoped he would be as successful at home.

Although the hot summer and overcrowding were over, the lice, graybacks as they were called, kept up their steady work. As one diarist wrote, "I tried to bear it but matters grew worse, till I hobbled out to a guard's fire nearby and begged a firebrand. Taking the blazing pitch pine brand and going back into the tent, I took off my clothes and killed over 400 graybacks by actual count. They were as large as a very large kernel of wheat, and the

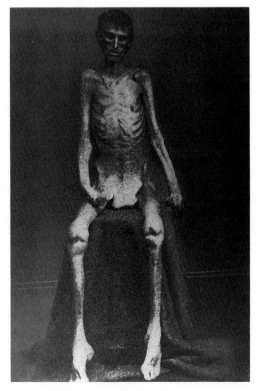

ANDERSONVILLE PRISONERS WHO HAD WASTED AWAY TO LIVING SKELETONS WERE PHOTOGRAPHED AFTER BEING EXCHANGED. THESE PHOTOS WERE LATER PUBLISHED IN NORTHERN NEWSPAPERS AND USED AS PROPAGANDA AGAINST THE SOUTH AND USED AS EVIDENCE TO HELP CONVICT CAPTAIN WIRZ.

(LC)

FORT DELAWARE

Fort Delaware prison was located on Pea Patch Island in the Delaware River. Approximately 33,565 Confederate prisoners passed through during its existence. The prison was constructed as a fort to protect northern cities. A 12-foot-deep, 30-foot moat surrounded the prison. The granite walls were seven to thirty feet thick. The prison was plagued with the usual diseases and malnutrition of all prisons north and south during the Civil War.

At this prison 2,436 Confederate prisoners died.

Their bodies were transported by boat to the New Jersey side of the Delaware River and buried in trenches at a place called Inns Point. A towering granite obelisk marks the spot and at its base are plaques with the names of the soldiers in the common grave.

(USAMHI)

1867 PHOTO SHOWS THE COVERED WAY, WITH THE MIDDLE STOCKADE ON THE RIGHT AND THE THIRD STOCKADE WALL ON THE LEFT.

(NA)

scars where they bit me I shall carry to the grave."

In the latter part of November, four or five wagon loads of vegetables were brought in by the citizens of nearby Americus. The vegetables were never distributed to the prisoners and were consumed by the authorities of the prison. In December the toll continued with 165 deaths. The grounds of the stockade looked like a battlefield with abandoned shebangs and items such as cups, canteens and worn-out clothing strewn throughout the grounds. It had been a battlefield in some sense. Many, many deaths occurred here as the nearby cemetery could testify. These men had not been torn apart by bullets but by loneliness, disease, malnutrition, filth and vermin. They didn't die fast but slowly, perhaps remembering their wives, children, mothers and fathers.

At the beginning of December 2,000 prisoners arrived from Salisbury, North Carolina. On December 22 in a letter to General Cooper, inspector general of the Confederacy, General Winder wrote, "Savannah evacuated. Had not the prisoners from Columbia, Salisbury and Florence better be removed immediately to Andersonville. Only one road now

CAMP FLORENCE

Camp Florence was located in Florence County, South Carolina and was one of the largest Southern Civil War prisons. The prison was 23 acres in size and was enclosed by a wall of logs 12 feet high. An embankment outside the wall stood three feet below the top of the wall and served as a walkway for the guards. No tents or shelters were furnished to the prisoners. Wood was left inside the stockade and the first arrivals used the wood for huts and cooking. Lack of adequate food, pure water, sanitation facilities and shelter was responsible for 20 deaths per day.

The prison was open for five months from September 1864 to February 1865. Between 15,000 and 18,000 Federal prisoners passed through the gates, and 2,802 died within the compound. Florence National Cemetery, in Florence, South Carolina, consists of 5 3/4 acres. Because the listing of the deaths was lost, there are 2,1167 unknowns.

(NPS)

open by way of Branchville to Augusta. I think there is not a moment to be lost. Please answer at once." General Winder would die of an apparent heart attack while on an inspection trip to Salisbury Prison on February 6, 1865.

As December 25 approached, Michael Daghtery, 13th Pennsylvania Cavalry, surely spoke for many of the prisoners when he wrote, "On Christmas Day thinking of our friends at home enjoying themselves, and how we are situated here, no rations of any kind. Little of our friends at home think we are in this situation. God grant them health to enjoy many more. This is my sincere wish to my poor mother and sister. I hope I will see them soon."

Prisoners were again arriving daily. It was cold and wet, a typical Georgia December. To beat the cold some would band into groups and lay next to each other all night and most of the day to stay warm. They would only leave this huddled mass to answer roll call and receive their rations. Graybacks could also interrupt their attempt at warmth. Private Lassel Long, 13th Indiana Infantry, related that,

October 23, 1864

As for myself, I never felt so utterly depressed, cursed, and God-for-saken in all my life before, All my former experiences in battles, on marches, and at my capture were not a drop in the bucket as compared with this.

Walter E. Smith Pvt., Co. K, 14th Illinois Infantry

THE BODIES WERE LAID TO REST SIDE BY SIDE IN SIX-FOOT WIDE BY THREE-FOOT DEEP TRENCHES. THIS PHOTO AT THE CEMETERY WAS TAKEN IN THE SUMMER OF 1864.

(NA)

*December 29,
1864*

*We sit around our
scanty fires shiv-
ering and hungry
thinking of what
good times we
might enjoy were
we permitted to
be at home. We
endeavor to keep
a stiff upper lip.*

*George M. Shearer
Private, Co. E, 17th
Iowa Infantry*

"As soon as we would begin to get a little warm they would commence their daily and nightly drill. They would have division, brigade, regiment, and company drills, ending up with a general review. When those large fellows began to prance around in front of the lines it would make some one halloo out, 'I must turn over, I can't stand this any longer.' So we would all turn to the right or left as the case might be. This would stop the chaps for a short time."

The new year claimed 197 deaths its first month. Four thousand to five thousand arrived from other prison camps during January with most of them occupying the south end of the prison. At the end of January, Captain Wirz complained about the prisoners stealing hospital property and selling it to the guards. There were also frequent escapes from the hospital. Wirz mentioned in a letter dated January 21 that a covered way and a third stockade wall had been started but asked whether this new stockade should be finished or the six-foot-high fence around the hospital be torn down and a real stockade built around the hospital to stop the stealing, trading and escapes. The covered way was never completed and a stockade around the hospital was never started.

According to historical documents the winter of 1864-1865 was the coldest winter in twenty-five years in southwest Georgia. One night the temperature was eighteen degrees above zero. The prisoners were poorly clad and the wood they attempted to burn for warmth was too wet to do much good. Toward the end of January more new prisoners were brought in. As Charles Fosdick wrote, "We old dried skeletons gathered around them in such great numbers that it is a wonder they did not get frightened to death at our ghostly appearance."

February began more pleasantly than the long cold month of January. The captives knew that if Sherman had been defeated there would have been a larger influx of prisoners. The only ones coming in were prisoners from other locations in the South. The weather broke with pleasant and warmer days. The prisoners took more exercise, and they even began to

THE EXECUTION OF HENRY WIRZ

Historians who have studied the tragic episode of Andersonville agree that even in the grip of understandable hysteria after President Abraham Lincoln's assassination, an indefensible travesty of justice was committed against Captain Henry Wirz. Worn and haggard, he was still at his post when Union Captain Henry E. Noyes arrived at Andersonville in early May with orders for his arrest. Noyes took Wirz to Washington where a military commission tried, convicted, and sentenced him to hang for: (1) conspiring with Jefferson Davis, Howell Cobb, John H., Richard B., and W.S. Winder, Isaiah H. White, R. Randolph Stevenson, and others to "Impair and injure the health and to destroy the lives... of large numbers of federal prisoners... at Andersonville" and (2) "murder, in violation of the laws and customs of war." Wirz was tried under these charges, convicted and sentenced to death. The sentence was carried out on November 10, 1865, on the courtyard of old Capitol Prison.

February 24, 1865

Our clothes were nearly worn out, and we had to go around and seek out the dead and rob them of the clothes they had in order to keep from freezing to death ourselves.

Bjorn Aslaksan

(LC)

sing patriotic songs. For the first time in twelve months the boys were optimistic. The rumors were good rumors: exchange, the end of the war, going home. Private Lassel Long wrote that a newly arrived prisoner made a speech to many of the prisoners saying, "I tell you this blasted rebellion cannot succeed. It was born in sin and cradled in iniquity, and it is going to pieces like a ship driven upon a rock. Bill Sherman is at this time cutting a swath through South Carolina forty miles wide." At this point the prisoners began cheering, and after they had cheered until they were hoarse, someone started up, "Rally around the flag, boys," then it was taken up all over the camp.

In March death still visited Andersonville Prison. One hundred and eight died, mostly prisoners in the hospital. Through the guards, prisoners learned that the Yankees had captured Selma, Alabama, and would soon be coming. New prisoners, and there were very few, brought only good news. Still, at Andersonville rations were just enough to keep the prisoners alive. On March 25, 800 prisoners left and there was talk that a train would leave every day full of prisoners. On March 28 new prisoners brought word that General Wilson's Cavalry was on the way.

In April the end of the war was in sight. Twenty-eight died during this last full month of Andersonville's existence. Most of the prisoners were sent to Vicksburg

March 7, 1865

In March, 1865, we began to hear rumors of the advance of our forces from the guards, and to look forward with hope to the time when we should once more be free.

Thadeus L. Waters Private, Co. G, 2nd Michigan Cav.

remembered, their experience never forgotten.

What became of the prisoners who left Andersonville? Hundreds perished on their way home when the steamboat they were on, the *Sultana*, exploded and sank near Memphis, Tennessee. Countless others died in northern hospitals, or in their hometowns of the diseases incurred during their captivity at Andersonville.

Over the years, the finger of blame has pointed in many directions, but the facts show that events of the time made this national tragedy happen. As the war dragged on and the exchange system collapsed, thousands of prisoners-of-war, Union and Confederate alike, found themselves in hastily constructed and poorly supplied prison camps. Many never returned to their homes, families or friends. At Andersonville human misery reached its zenith. The tombstones in Andersonville National Cemetery and the written words of the prisoners tell a tragic story.

for exchange. Slowly but surely the prisoners left Andersonville. When Union forces finally arrived at Andersonville in May, about three weeks after the war had ended, only a small number of prisoners remained. Arrangements were made to transport these sick and frail soldiers home. While the prisoners waited, Andersonville claimed its last victim.

It was over. The ground now was bare of the living. Where only a short time before had been masses of living and dying there was now an assortment of discarded blankets, handmade cooking utensils and worn-out clothing. In only fourteen months, 12,914 had died on this ground. Their sacrifice will always be